Bringing Down The Sky

haiku by

Steven B. Harvey

Finishing Line Press
Georgetown, Kentucky

Bringing Down The Sky

For my wife Allison, my poem of poems

Copyright © 2019 by Steven B. Harvey
ISBN 978-1-63534-862-0 First Edition
All rights reserved under International and Pan-American Copyright Conventions.
No part of this book may be reproduced in any manner whatsoever without written permission from the publisher, except in the case of brief quotations embodied in critical articles and reviews.

Publisher: Leah Maines
Editor: Christen Kincaid
Cover Art: Steven B. Harvey
Author Photo: Jennifer Girard Photography
Cover Design: Leah Huete

Printed in the USA on acid-free paper.
Order online: www.finishinglinepress.com
          also available on amazon.com

                  Author inquiries and mail orders:
                        Finishing Line Press
                            P. O. Box 1626
                      Georgetown, Kentucky 40324
                                U. S. A.

Table of Contents

In Red Ink ix

Summer 1

Autumn 7

Winter 13

Spring 19

In Red Ink

The cardinal's syrup song slides through the crack of dawn

Summer

The sky is swollen
My body thinks about you
The release of rain

On the red river
One blue true forget-me-not
Is there forever

The green of that tree
Against the blue of that sky
Is impossible

Summer's twilight sky
My daughter swings and I pray
Our hands on heaven

Thunder is awake
Our daughter commands the storm
Her rain is silver

You are my weather
I sail on your shining face
Anchor on your sleep
A fresh breeze pursued by rain
Now we begin our voyage

Cicada chorus
Their electric prophecy
Tomorrow again

My daughter's body
Leaf resting on an old bough
Dancing on my breath

After a long drought
A rain stingy as your love
Leaves us parched

Autumn

November cloud hunt
An arrow of seven geese
Bringing down the sky

Emblems of autumn
Leaves at our feet startle us
So far from the sky

Fall's beckoning sky
Of unbelievable blue
Awakening me

Red November dawn
Bottoms of grey clouds aflame
In pools on the ground

At my desk I dream
Of the silent golden wood
Your voice on each leaf

In the golden wood
Leaves sinking in the silent air
Weigh upon your words

Millions of leaves fall
Becoming one another
I hold the real one

In a silver rain
Last leaves fly like golden flags
Autumn blows away

Thousands of autumns
Millions of leaves have fallen
This leaf never fell

Leaves give up the sky
Hills become a million suns
Heaven on the earth

Grey geese departing
Through ribs of a falling sky
The cold mouth of dawn

Our honey locust
So discrete until autumn
When it lights the sky

Winter

A cricket last night
Unmindful of December
A fool in his song

Taken by surprise
A larger hand seeking mine
My daughter's growing

Late in bed today
With no luxury of sleep
And dread of waking

First day of winter
Birds at my window sing
Happy and sad songs

First snowfall tonight
One body's print in my sheet
I listen for you

Winter's still garden
Where I surprised you last spring
Awakened by life

We parted in spring
I hungered through summer
Burned all winter

jewel blue morning
Winter wrought black filigree
A tree before the sky

First day of the year
The prospect of meeting you
Brings me a good dream

Spring

Willow becoming
Gauzy green April twilight
Visible again

April's surprise snow
Sheaths sliding from crocus stalks
To sun stained earth

The fly on our porch
Declaring that it's April
Months ahead of me

I found your letter
Among old forgotten things
Your love made me smile

March recedes on winds
Broken wings of umbrellas
Flail on floating buds

Pools of April rain
Bring the blue sky to the ground
Gulls walk on white clouds

Spring jumps the train tracks
An arc of electric blue
A jay takes the sky

I should be reading
April blooms with no regard
The day says see now

Spring night in your arms
The next day you forget me
Do I still exist

The bird of your mouth
Flies to my throat and captures
Words I might have said

Hard to imagine
Myself aged forty-eight
My heart feeling new

March blows grey and gold
Undecided about spring
Snow falls to flowers

Birds sing a sweet wind
Up the river in April
Buds burst swaying boughs

Steven **Harvey** is a poet and sculptor living and working in Chicago. After leaving university with a degree in Philosophy and Fine Arts, Steven worked as a tool and die maker, a director of marketing for a consumer products manufacturing firm, an independent marketing consultant and as an account executive and market analyst for some of the leading equities and futures firms. He has been creating poetry and exhibiting sculpture since the late 60's. His sculpture has received cash awards and grant funding and has been represented by some of Chicago's top galleries. His work is in private and corporate collections. Steven has been working in long form poetry as well as the shorter forms represented here. He is currently completing a collection of these long form works.

www.ingramcontent.com/pod-product-compliance
Lightning Source LLC
LaVergne TN
LVHW041515070426
835507LV00012B/1585